ZOË

ZOË

AN INTRODUCTION TO THE TRANSCENDENT LIFE

ADAM C. J. DYESS

Contributor: Collier D. Robertson

Grace Publishing

to my father,
who taught me to ask questions

This is eternal life:
that they may know You, the only true God,
and the One You have sent — Jesus Christ.
- John 17:3

Telescopes are a wonderful thing. With less than $200, you can buy one that will allow you to see the rings on Saturn! Thousands of years ago, the ancient Greeks looked at the stars without the advantage of magnification and were still able to map out multitudes of stars. In their exploration, they observed that there were basically two types of stars: fixed stars and stars that wandered. The former were obviously helpful in understanding time and position. But what about those wandering stars? They looked similar, but you couldn't easily use them to navigate. Thus, these moving stars were called 'Planao' which means 'wandering' or 'deceiving.' From this root, we get the word *planet*. Though we understand now why planets move independent of the stars, we still refer to them as *wandering*. This word, 'planao' appears in the New Testament several times.

Matt 24:4

Watch out that no one deceives (planao) you...

2 Timothy 3:12-13

In fact, all those who want to live a godly life in Christ Jesus will be persecuted. Evil people and impostors will become worse, deceiving (planao) and being deceived (planao).

In other words, we are warned about the wandering deceptions of the world that will multiply confusion and foolishness. The solution is to keep your attention focused on the One who is fixed and unchanging. In our study together, we will help you answer some of the deepest questions that everyone faces. As we discover these answers, you may notice the difference between the world's way (planao or *wandering*) and the Way of Jesus (eternal).

HOW TO READ THIS BOOK (*Warning*)

In examining the following four questions (Who am I? Where did I come from? Why am I here? Where am I going?), we are going to explore what it means to embrace the call from Jesus to "follow Me" and experience the gift of eternal life. These questions are fundamental to all people throughout history. While countless philosophers and religious gurus have tried to press in to understand, they all fell short in one way or another. That is, until Jesus entered the pages of history. What He lived and taught is what we will discover, and ultimately, draw near to God as a result. While we take this journey together, we will also seek out 4 virtues (one at the end of each chapter): Prayer, Worship,

Study, and Witness. Take time in between lessons to practice these virtues. Now here is the warning: If you seek the LORD during this time, you will not be the same when you complete this book. You must be warned that as you progress, many of the habits you enjoy will be called out. The idols that might lurk beneath the surface will appear, and some will be offended. This book is not for entertainment. It is for discipleship. When you are challenged, you must decide if you will surrender or harden your heart.

Before we proceed, let us consider this excerpt from the prayer of Jesus in the garden before His arrest.

> **John 17:3**
> *This is eternal life:*
> *that they may know You*
> *the only true God, and the One You have sent,*
> *Jesus Christ*

When Jesus was praying to the Father in heaven that night, he declared that eternal life is KNOWING GOD. This seems unusual at first because we have always heard that eternal life is a place in heaven far away. This will make sense in just a moment. But first, let's examine the word KNOW. The initial impression is that *know* means some kind of intellectual understanding of a set of facts or ideas. However, the bible uses this word in a much more personal way. Consider the day that you first learned how to ride a bicycle. There was a sudden rush of exhilaration as you wobbled down the road and the wind brushed your face. All of your muscles began to work together. You fell a few more times, but soon everything became natural. You *knew* how to ride a bike. Notice that this type of knowing cannot occur until it is experienced. You may sit in plenty of bicycle learning classes for hours and grasp the mechanics and physical principles that are at play, but you still cannot say that you *know* how to ride a bike until you *ride the bike*. Knowing implies relationship, experience, and intimacy. Now back to the subject of eternal life.

Eternal life not so much a *place* as it is a relationship with a Person. Another analogy will help here. Imagine for a moment you are planning your honeymoon with the love of your life. You discover at the last moment you have two options: 1. go to the place of your dreams but *without* your spouse. 2. go somewhere else *with* your spouse. Obviously, you will take option 2. You just got married and you want to be with your spouse! The thought of going on a honeymoon without this other person is absurd. In fact, it almost doesn't even matter where you go, as long as you are together. It's not about being on a tropical island; it's about being *with* the other person. When we learn that marriage is itself a symbol of the relationship between God and His people (Ephesians 5:31-32), then the picture of eternal life starts to come into focus. Would you want to go to heaven if God was not there? Is heaven even heaven without God's presence? No, certainly not. In fact, it is clear that heaven IS the presence of God. In his autobiography, *Surprised by Joy*, C. S. Lewis recounts this startling discovery. As a young boy, Lewis had an intuition that the deepest desire of his heart was a mystical island far away. What he came to realize was that what he longed for was, in fact, a Person and not a Place. Now here is some good news. We can begin to explore this Personal relationship with God today! You do not have to wait until you are standing before Him. Eternal life can be explored the moment we put our trust in Christ and His work.

Now, one more word on the word LIFE. There are three Greek words that are all translated as *life* in one place or another in the New Testament. The first one is the word BIOS. In every place that this word is used, it refers to the things of this world which are passing away. It can sometimes refer to physical life and it is the root of the word Biology (see Luke 8:14, 1 Peter 4:3, 2 Timothy 2:4). The second word is PSYCHE. This word refers to the human soul and is manifested as *will, emotion,* and *mind.* Sometimes, this word is translated as soul such as (insert verse). PSYCHE (pronounced *soo-keh)* is the root word for Psychology (see Matthew 6:25, Matthew 16:25, Acts 15:26, Romans 11:3). The third word that is translated as life is the word ZOE. This word uniquely refers to the transcendent life that is in God which animates and sustains creation. For example, when Jesus says "I am the Way, the Truth, and the *Life"* (John 14:6), he is using the word ZOE. In other words, there is a type of life that goes beyond what we know in this world. Which of these three words do you think Jesus uses in the prayer in John 17:3? It is ZOE! This is life everlasting (see John 3:16, John 10:10, Matthew 7:14, Philippians 4:3).

Let us begin.

Adam Dyess
Grace MBC, Pastor

Three Greek words for LIFE

3 Greek Words in the New Testament translated as *life*

1. Bios: the life and living of *this* world and physical life.

    And that which fell among thorns are they, which, when they have heard, go forth, and are choked with cares and riches and pleasures of this **life**, and bring no fruit to perfection. - **Luke 8:14**

    For the time past of our **life** may suffice us to have wrought the will of the Gentiles, when we walked in lasciviousness, lusts, excess of wine, revellings, banquetings, and abominable idolatries: - **1 Peter 4:3**

    No man that warreth entangleth himself with the affairs of this **life**; that he may please him who hath chosen him to be a soldier. - **2 Timothy 2:4**

2. Psyche: the human soulish existence manifested as will, emotion, and mind.

    For whosoever will save his **life** shall lose it: and whosoever will lose his **life** for my sake shall find it. - **Matthew 16:25**

Lord, they have killed thy prophets, and digged down thine altars; and I am left alone, and they seek my **life.** - **Romans 11:3**

Men that have hazarded their **lives** for the name of our Lord Jesus Christ. - **Acts 15:26** .

3. Zoe - the eternal transcendent life that is in God, animating and sustaining creation.

Because strait is the gate, and narrow is the way, which leadeth unto **life**, and few there be that find it.
- **Matthew 7:14**

And if thy hand offend thee, cut it off: it is better for thee to enter into **life** maimed, than having two hands to go into hell, into the fire that never shall be quenched: - **Mark 9:43**

For God so loved the world, that he gave his only begotten Son, that whosoever believeth in him should not perish, but have everlasting **life.** – **John 3:16**

The thief cometh not, but for to steal, and to kill, and to destroy: I am come that they might have **life**, and that they might have it more abundantly. - **John 10:10**

Jesus saith unto him, I am the way, the truth, and the **life**: no man cometh unto the Father, but by me. - **John 14:6**

And I intreat thee also, true yokefellow, help those women which laboured with me in the gospel, with Clement also, and with other my fellowlabourers, whose names are in the book of **life**. - **Philippians 4:3**

1

IDENTITY: Who am I?

"Your name will no longer be Jacob," He said. *"It will be Israel"*
Genesis 32:28a

An Old Story

Jacob, which means 'heel-grabber' or 'supplanter', lived up to his name in many respects. Jacob was always scheming and plotting. He lied to his father, tricked his brother, and tried to get around an ancient custom by marrying a younger daughter before the older was married. In the third case, Jacob's plan failed dramatically, but that wasn't the point. The point was that he wrestled his way through life in his own strength. That is, until he wrestled with God.

The Name Game

Even before we learn to speak, there is an identity crisis that begins to form internally. You can see the inquisitive look on an infant's face as they discover their own reflection. Though it starts very early, the quest of *self* is a lifelong journey. Unsurprisingly, when we seek for a single answer, we receive a multitude. These identities manifest as *names*. Read the following and see if you notice something familiar.

I am my job *(I am a doctor, teacher, college student)*
I am my hobbies *(I am a collector. I am a gamer)*
I am my successes *(I am a graduate. I am a winner.)*
I am my failures *(I am a drop-out. I am a loser)*
I am what they say about me *(I am stupid. I am ugly)*
I am my hopes/dreams *(I am a hero. I am a traveler)*
I am my fears *(I am alone. I am unwanted)*
I am my physical appearance *(I am attractive. I am fat)*
I am my talents/abilities *(I am a musician. I am an athlete)*
I am my disabilities *(I am ADHD. I am a dyslexic.)*

What is a name?

Our search for identity is an old one. From the dawn of human language, we have expressed our understanding of things by giving names. To name something is to give it identity. In the story of creation in Genesis, Adam is given the command to name all the animals. This authority is carried on today in almost every area of society. We name the planets, the mountains, the buildings, the cars, etc.; but most significantly, we exercise this sacred privilege in the naming of our children. In all the confusion over naming and being named, one might wonder why names are even necessary. Why can't things just be what they want to be? And then, a startling insight emerges:

We must be told who we are.

This may not sound too bad at first, but then we remember that as we grow, many times what we are told is harmful:

> A woman in an abusive relationship begins to think
> ...I *am* unworthy.
> A boy bullied on the playground begins to believe
> ...I *am* a reject.
> A girl with a neglectful father says to herself
> ...I *am* unlovable.
> A student who receives a bad report starts to assume
> ...I *am* stupid.

So what do we do with this dilemma?`

One Bad Answer: ***Deconstructionism***

There is a cynical philosophy packaged in a deceptively well-meaning mantra. Often repeated in our culture, the response to taking on a false label from others, is this: *assert your own identity*. Recently, Vice President Kamala Harris was asked by a group of children to give her most important piece of advice. Here was her response:

"I want you to really remember this. Never let anybody tell you who you are. You tell them who you are."[1]

Can you spot the problem?

Initially, the logic looks good. We can reject the negative labels by rejecting all of them. Of course, the false and destructive names should be dismantled. But where does it stop?

Why should parents have the right to name their children?
Why shouldn't children just name themselves?
What does a teacher know about the "grade" of their student?
What is a woman?
What is a criminal?
Why should a gender "assignment" be binding?
What is "personal property"?
What is truth?

Deconstructionism always dissolves into **social relativism**. This philosophy is dangerous because it ultimately rejects the authority of God and His Good Order. It mimics the words of the serpent in the garden, "you will be like God."[2]

1 *https://www.youtube.com/watch?v=U5PABXXdDwA&ab_channel=TheTelegraph [:18]*
2 Gen. 3:5

So what is the truth?

The answer, surprisingly, begins with a biblical understanding of light.

John 1:5
That light shines in the darkness,
yet the darkness did not overcome it.

A Biblical Perspective: Light and Darkness

When light floods into a room, there is no battle with darkness. Light simply casts out the dark. The same can be said for spiritual light, or enlightenment. Like a man who wakes up from a deep sleep and immediately sees through the illusion of the dream, so too the man who receives the epiphany of revelation. Jon writes about that *light* that came into the world. However, the problem lies with those who *want* to stay asleep, even when the sun breaks in through the window.

> John 3:19
> *This, then, is the judgment: The light has come into the world, and people loved darkness rather than the light because their deeds were evil.*

Many years ago, when I was still in elementary school, there was a day like no other. I came home from school on the bus, interested in completing a homework assignment. I remember standing in a bedroom holding my paper but still in need of a pencil. It's important here to explain that our family was poor. In fact, we had nearly everything jerry rigged at our house. In the middle bedroom, there was a single incandescent light bulb hanging on live wires that dangled from the ceiling. There was a dark closet full of clothes and other random objects on the floor. Two thoughts entered my mind. First, in search of a pencil, I hypothesized that there might be one somewhere in the closet. The second thought turned out to be much more consequential. I looked up at the lightbulb and pondered if I could somehow move it lower so that I could see into the closet. Now, you probably know that when a man has made up his mind, even a young man, there's no sense trying to reason with him. I climbed up on the bed post and reached as high as I could. This turned out to be just high enough to lift the mangled light fixture off the wire hooks. *Eureka!* Oh wait, the lightbulb was no longer lit. But it was still very hot; hot enough for me to fall on to the bed with the bulb now sitting on the corner of the mattress. I was *struck down but not destroyed* (let the reader understand). The thing I shall never quite comprehend is just how motivated I was to complete this assignment. I searched in the darkness of the closet, now made even darker by the sudden absence of the room light. For several minutes, I rummaged through random piles of stuff. Because of what happened next, I cannot tell you if I stopped searching because I found a pencil or because I accepted defeat. But at this point, I turned back around and noticed that the light bulb was sitting much lower. *Curious.* Upon removing the light from the bed, my eyes gazed into the newly formed hole on the corner of the mattress. Fear and panic stabbed my chest. There was only one thing to do: Quickly return everything in the room to normal, throw the blanket on the bed to hide the evidence, and escape to the living room and TV.

Time went by. Eventually, my father returned from work, tired and wanting to nap...

My memory is somewhat foggy here. I remember a bellowing scream. And in the next image, I am standing in the hallway, watching my dad run back and forth between the room and the bathroom with a bucket of water, pouring it into the hole and elsewhere on the mattress. Violent threatenings about what would soon occur echoed through the hallway. There was thunder and lightning. The bed was literally on fire. It was a fearful day.

I won't speak about the initial aspirations that I had that day, or the woeful education I received about basic physics. Rather, let us consider what is common in the story to us all: the fearful hiding from the truth.

> *Jn. 3:19*
> *light has come into the world, and people loved darkness rather than the light because their deeds were evil.*

This is the story of every man. It goes all the way back to the first one. Adam hid in the fig leaves of the garden. We don't want to be *found out.* Or, to put it bluntly, we don't want to be *found.* But that must mean, then, that we *are* lost.

In searching for identity, the first step to take is to come to terms with the state of affairs. A lost man cannot find his own way.

On the contrary, the answer must come through the lens of revelation. If a man really is *lost*, what hope does he have of discovering his true self on his own terms?

Lost on Purpose

> Jeremiah 17:9 (KJV)
> *The heart is deceitful above all things, and desperately wicked: who can know it?*

We are worse than *merely* lost. We are lost *on purpose*. We are *rebels*. A rebel cannot find God the same way a criminal cannot find the police. He runs like an insect away from the light. To him, the light is only pain and exposure. There is a strange sense of comfort, however temporary, in the company of darkness, even if it is poisonous. Darkness doesn't judge or uncover. One can befriend darkness for a season and find relief. Yet, the relief is shallow and bitter. Misery whispers in the recesses *hello.* Like a python, darkness quietly strangles its prey and slowly devours it.

On the other hand, light comes in swift like a sword. Painful at first, but for those who humble themselves, light is a surgeon's blade that cuts *deeply* and *carefully*.

John 3:17
For God did not send His Son into the world that He might condemn the world, but that the world might be saved through Him.

The question before us is now presented.

Will you allow the Light of God to tell you who you are?

A New Name

Let's consider a man in the New Testament named Simon. Simon was a man that often spoke too soon and too much. He was a man who put a lot of faith in himself and in his abilities. Having not made the cut in religious school, Simon was, like many others, destined to take on the family business. Then one day, Simon met Jesus, and Jesus immediately gave Simon a new name:

John 1:42
And he brought Simon to Jesus. When Jesus saw him, He said, "You are Simon, son of John. You will be called Cephas" (which means "Rock").

From that point on, Jesus challenged Simon to follow Him on a mission of identity, and, in the process, Simon discovered a remarkable truth:

When we know who God is, we discover who we are.

As Jesus popularity rose, so did the rumors of Jesus' own identity. In one very important conversation, Jesus asked His disciples to answer a question not about who they were, but who Jesus is.

> Matthew 16:15-18
> *"But you," He asked them, "who do you say that I am?" Simon Peter answered, "You are the Messiah, the Son of the living God!" And Jesus responded, "Simon son of Jonah, you are blessed because flesh and blood did not reveal this to you, but My Father in heaven. And I also say to you that you are Peter, and on this rock I will build My church, and the forces of Hades will not overpower it.*

Did you notice that after Simon confesses Jesus as the Messiah and the Son of the living God, Jesus affirms Simon's name as *Peter*.

Our true identity is interwoven with our understanding of God *and His love for us.*

God gives a name to His children that reflects the spiritual transformation that occurs from knowing God for who He is (ie: Jacob to Israel, Abram to Abraham, Simon to Peter, etc). This renaming signifies a new identity. When we put our trust in Jesus as the Son of the Living God, we receive a new name.

Our identity goes from:

Broken   *to*   Restored
Sinner   *to*   Saint
Lost   *to*   Found
Dead   *to*   Living
Wicked   *to*   Righteous

Child of Wrath   *to*   Child of God

Your name changes from **CURSED** to **CHRISTIAN**!

1 Corinthians 6:9-11

*Don't you know that the unrighteous will not inherit God's kingdom? Do not be deceived: No sexually immoral people, idolaters, adulterers, or anyone practicing homosexuality, no thieves, greedy people, drunkards, verbally abusive people, or swindlers will inherit God's kingdom. And some of you used to be like this. **But you were washed**, you were **sanctified**, you were **justified** in the name of the Lord Jesus Christ and by the Spirit of our God.*

And just like that, hydra is felled. The thousands of false identities are cast away by the presence of God's Spirit.

Romans 8:15-16

For you did not receive a spirit of slavery to fall back into fear, but you received the Spirit of adoption, by whom we cry out, "Abba, Father!" The Spirit Himself testifies together with our spirit that we are God's children

To summarize, natural identity is warped by sin. Disobedience and confusion mark the carnal man. He is in a covenant with darkness. However, True Light, in the Person of Jesus, has come into the world, rescuing all who are willing. Anyone who undergoes the knife of the Great Physician will also enter into a new covenant with light. As a consequence, he will awaken to his true identity. He *is* who God has made him to be.

So far, we have left out the central mechanism for the power behind this transformation. The short answer is that this is all made possible by the work of Jesus **on the cross.** The gospel is the death, burial, and resurrection of Jesus, on our behalf. When Jesus died, He conquered the powers of sin and death. And, for all who have received this gift by faith, the carnal nature is crucified *with Him.* By Jesus' death, that old nature, deceitful and condemned, is slain. By Jesus' Resurrection, the new man is born.

> **Galatians 2:19-20**
> *For through the law I have died to the law, so that I might live for God. I have been crucified with Christ and I no longer live, but Christ lives in me. The life I now live in the body, I live by faith in the Son of God, who loved me and gave Himself for me.*

> **2 Corinthians 5:17**
> *Therefore if anyone is in Christ, he is a new creation; old things have passed away, and look, new things have come.*

In Christ, you are given *eternal* life, a *true* identity, and a *new* name. But what does this look like?

A Saint

Colossians 1:12-13
*Giving thanks to the Father, who has enabled you to **share in the saints' inheritance** in the light. 13 He has rescued us from the domain of darkness and transferred us into the kingdom of the Son He loves.*

Ephesians 2:19
*Now therefore ye are no more strangers and foreigners, but fellowcitizens **with the saints**, and of the household of God*

Paul uses the word 'saints' initially to describe the fellowship of Jewish believers in Jerusalem. They had received their Messiah Jesus and obtained eternal life through His blood. A saint is simply someone who is *of the people of God.*

Here in these passages, Paul describes an extension of sainthood to all believers, Jew or Gentile. We are invited to share in the inheritance of those saints, and so we are named among them. Thus, the word *Christian* and the word *Saint* become somewhat interchangeable. Don't worry, you don't have to perform three miracles to be considered a saint!

A Son

John 1:12-13

But as many as received him, to them gave he power to become the sons of God, even to them that believe on his name: Which were born, not of blood, nor of the will of the flesh, nor of the will of man, but of God (KJV)

Romans 8:15-16

For you did not receive a spirit of slavery to fall back into fear, but you received the Spirit of adoption, by whom we cry out, "Abba, Father!" The Spirit Himself testifies together with our spirit that we are God's children

Even though all humanity has been created by God, sin has orphaned us. This means that, by nature, we belong more to the devil than we do to God (John 8:44). The bible also refers to man as *children of disobedience* (Col. 3:6) and *children of wrath* (Eph. 2:3). Through the gospel, believers have been adopted into the family of God and are now treated as *sons*. Some translations may use the word *children* more often; however, the Greek implies a child with a birthright. This is because the consequence of adoption is more than just a relationship. It includes inheritance!

Romans 8:16-17

The Spirit Himself testifies together with our spirit that we are God's children, and if children, also heirs — heirs of God and co-heirs with Christ — seeing that we suffer with Him so that we may also be glorified with Him.

The beauty of God adopting us into his family is that it reflects His goodness, not our rights! We have no inherent merit or value that allows us to be a part of God's family. It is by his grace towards us and his love for us that we are accepted and brought in. As a son of God, you are no longer a slave to your sin, or a lost and wandering orphan, but an *heir of God* and *co-heir with Christ!* Therefore, your identity is found not in yourself, but in the fact that you are a son of God and an heir, receiving the promises and blessings from God the Father because of his love for you. This means that your identity never changes or alters. It isn't based on your perfect faithfulness, but on the perfect faithfulness of God.

Not only are we adopted as Children of God into his household, but we have been given the right to be called Jesus' brother!

> ### Hebrews 2:11-12
> *For the One who sanctifies and those who are sanctified all have one Father. That is why Jesus is not ashamed to call them brothers, saying "I will proclaim Your name to My brothers"*

This passage of scripture gives a beautiful picture of what Jesus has done for us so that we may be called His brothers and sons of God. Jesus gave up His glory with the Father, became lower than the angels for a time, and suffered so that we might have victory over death through Him. Because of His death and merciful sacrifice, we are able to become **saints** and **sons**.

There is much to say about the subject of prayer, but to keep it simple for now, prayer is the communication between you and God. There will be many things that attempt to control your time, so you must be active in protecting your own prayer life. In Psalm 63, David describes the passion that he has in seeking God personally. If remain passive toward prayer, it will become shallow and barren. If your schedule is so demanding that you are too busy to pray, change your schedule and prioritize your relationship with God. Remember that you will never have more freedom than you do right now. If you cannot pray today, tomorrow will be no easier.

Psalm 63:1-8

God, You are my God; I eagerly seek You. I thirst for You; my body faints for You in a land that is dry, desolate, and without water. So I gaze on You in the sanctuary to see Your strength and Your glory.

My lips will glorify You because Your faithful love is better than life. So I will praise You as long as I live; at Your name, I will lift up my hands. You satisfy me as with rich food; my mouth will praise You with joyful lips.

When I think of You as I lie on my bed, I meditate on You during the night watches because You are my helper; I will

Many Christians *want* to pray, but they do not know how to pray. In giving what is the most well-known prayer of all time, Jesus gave us a model of prayer. While we look at **Matthew 6:9-13,** observe 3 simple steps to praying that you can remember and apply today.

Step 1**: Acknowledge** - *Our Father who is in Heaven*

The first thing Jesus instructs about prayer is to express a proper understanding of God and our relationship to Him. First, God is *our Father*. Jesus could have said many words like King, Judge, Creator. But He said *Father*. Also, He describes God as *our* Father, not just His Father. It's so important to know when we pray, we are coming to a loving Father, not a distant autocrat.

Step 2: **Adore** - *Holy is Your Name. Your Kingdom come, Your Will be done*

Before getting into any concerns, Jesus invites us to *adore God*. We recognize and marvel at His Holiness and Worthiness. Holy means *otherness*. There is no one truly like God. His Kingdom and His Will is better then anything man can come up with.

Step 3. **Ask** - *Give us this day, our daily bread, and forgive us our debts as we forgive our debtors. Lead us not into temptation but deliver us from the evil one.*

Notice that we are to ask for even the simple things, the modest things. Pour your heart out to Him for He cares for you! Part of this asking includes confession, for we ask for forgiveness. Seek God honestly and He will answer.

ACKNOWLEDGE. ADORE. ASK.

2

ORIGIN: Where did I come from?

*Be careful that no one takes you captive through philosophy
and empty deceit based on human tradition, based on the
elemental forces of the world, and not based on Christ.*
Colossians 2:8

Empty Human Philosophy

The common assumption to the question of our origin goes
something like this: We came from nothing significant; nothing
at all actually. Nothing spontaneously gave rise to everything,
and, at first, everything was pretty dull and boring, for *billions
of years*. And then, almost as spontaneous as the beginning, the
lifeless motion gave rise to something called *life*. This extremely

rudimentary life was so simple, it was almost indistinguishable from the nonlife surrounding it. Over the course of the next *billions of years*, this *simple* life gradually became more interesting and complex for no objective reason, other than in response to the environment. To put it bluntly, human beings came from some life form decidedly less conscious or valuable, which itself came from pure chemistry. Consequently, many people walk around today believing that their own sense of worth or importance is an illusion, and whatever notions of morality that have emerged in their hearts or in society are *purely* subjective. How does this sound? We must point out that this answer is not false merely because it is less desirable. It is false because it lacks explanatory power, contradicts reason, and does not agree with the deeper intuition that we all share. Or more simply, it is false because it is false. It is also important to remember that we ask the question "Where did I come from?" precisely because we perceive at some level that there is a full answer to it. If the answer provided does not satisfy the search, it has failed. Thus, the common answer is not an answer at all. It is a distraction and a lie that says 'you are only asking the question because of some biological phenomenon.'

So we come back to the beginning. Where *did* we come from? Perhaps unsurprisingly, we find the answer given briefly on the first page of the book of Genesis.

The Real Origin Story

Genesis 1:26-27

Then God said, "Let Us make man in Our image, according to Our likeness. They will rule the fish of the sea, the birds of the sky, the livestock, all the earth, and the creatures that crawl on the earth." So God created man in His own image; He created him in the image of God; He created them male and female.

To put it in a few words, man was created by God out of His abundant Power and Love. We are made *by* Him, we are made *for* Him, and we are drawn *to* Him. Therefore, our experiences of love, knowledge, and truth, are more than mere epistemological phenomena. These experiences and intuitions are derivatives of God's Nature that point us back to Him. What a wonderful idea!

Colossians 1:16-17

For everything was created by Him, in heaven and on earth, the visible and the invisible, whether thrones or dominions or rulers or authorities—all things have been created through Him and for Him. He is before all things, and by Him all things hold together.

So now, you might start to wonder, if God is the Source behind creation: *Who is this God that made us?*

Ontologically, God is the Uncreated, Self-sufficient Creator. There's a lot to unpack but let us begin by starting with what we can observe.

General Revelation

Romans 1:19

since what can be known about God is evident among them, because God has shown it to them. For His invisible attributes, that is, His eternal power and divine nature, have been clearly seen since the creation of the world, being understood through what He has made. As a result, people are without excuse.

General Revelation includes:

    a. Examination of nature (Natural Sciences)
    b. Examination of logic and introspection (Philosophy)

From this inquiry, we can derive that God exists, and we can learn something about His Nature. He is Eternal, Omnipotent, Intelligent, and is the source of Goodness, Beauty, and Truth.

We can start this pursuit by taking note of what our direct senses are saying. ***Je pense, donc je suis***[3] (*I think, therefore I am*) said Descartes, and perhaps, rightly so. If we *are*, what else *is?*

The world around us is clearly much bigger and full of wonder and mystery. Some of the mystery includes a deep longing and groaning in the heart of man and in the heart of the earth. As beautiful as everything is, it is also seemingly broken.

---

3 Descartes, René, *A Discourse on Method: Meditations and Principles,* 1637. Part IV

Despair, death, and misery seem to indicate that something is deeply *wrong* with the world.

Abstract concepts like numbers provide an interesting insight into a world beyond mere matter. The field of mathematics has had both profound impact on the technical and philosophical advancement of human civilization. One of the main reasons for this is the inexplicable dependability and applicability of Math in every direction of the observable universe. Why does math seem to work everywhere? It is as though Nature were telling us that some *One* beyond the Universe is keeping everything in order. This *One*, is both Supremely Powerful, and pays careful attention to detail. One surely bizarre fact of our investigation into the universe is that it is extremely big, if not infinite ($>10^{29}$ meters).[4] On the other end of the spectrum, the smallest *thing* we can measure is *extremely* small (10^{-36} meters).[5] This simple observation produces a profound mystery: Man finds himself right near the middle of everything. What could explain this? Perhaps, as some cosmologists and mathematicians speculate with fear and trepidation, the universe is truly infinite. Ok, what's the problem with that? The answers are many. First of all, with a truly infinite universe, not only is everything *possible,* everything *is.* This would mean there are, among the endless sea of universe potentials, infinite copies of you.

4 *The smallest measurement is a Planck Length: https://www.fnal.gov/pub/today/archive/ archive_2013/today13-11-01_NutshellReadMore.html*

5 *For a good article on minimum size of a finite universe: https://medium.com/starts-with-a-bang/ how-big-is-the-entire-universe-f3fdd468d3db*

Infinite versions of reality that are identical would be scattered across the cosmos. Not only that, infinite versions of reality just like this, but with indescribable modifications. For example, there would be a version of reality where in the next moment after reading this, you look up see a balloon the size of a city with baby elephants crawling on it. And literally anything else you can imagine. Things would happen that would defy our understanding of physics. This would be because, in an infinite universe (or multiverse), there are no *laws*. Any relative consistencies would be almost like anomalies among a chaotic ocean of contradictions. In fact, there would be way more of the noise than any semblance of an intelligible universe. So, now you should ask: What are the chances that you are in that minute percentage of areas in the infinite universe with *constants* that *seem* totally consistent?

This is just one of the problems with an infinite universe, and it's why so many have searched for some measurable degree of curvature in the skies. If there was even a tiny curve in space, positive or negative, then that would likely prove that the universe is finite. Similar problems emerge when you consider the Boltzmann brain thought experiment[6], which demonstrates the almost mathematical certainty that we do not exist as separate individuals living on a planet, but rather, all of your experiences and memories are merely illusions of random quantum fluctuations of gases that have converged to simulate a brain floating in space that just thinks that it is you.

6 *https://www.themarginalian.org/2022/12/05/boltzmann-brain-paradox/*

Apparently, there are way more of those out there than actual *yous*. What seems more likely? That you exist as a simulation in a marvel-themed multiverse? Or, it is more likely that this Universe is *positioned* in such a way that intelligent life flourishes somewhere right in the middle of things. It is possible that *Nature* is telling us that this world is *created* so that man can explore it and, through that exploration, come to know the *Being* that transcends it?

But if God created us, who created Him?

This question is often lobbed as an attack against Christian faith and the bible. Assuming though, that it is asked sincerely, one might initially see the logic in such a thought. After all, everything that we see was made something else, and so it stands to reason that this principle would apply to God. Critics will suggest that claiming that the universe was made by God is just moving the goal post because one could protest in the following way:

> **Critic:** 'If God made everything, *who* made God?'
> **Christian:** 'No one made God. He has always been'
> **Critic:** 'What a double standard! If something can be eternal, why can't we just say that the universe has always been and be done with it!'

This typical conversation underscores the profound misunderstanding about the clear difference between the universe and God. The reason we cannot say that universe has always been, is because it is *material,* and material entities have been shown to *begin* to exist.

Consider the following argument:

1. We, along with the universe, exist.
2. The entire material universe began to exist at some finite point in the past.
3. Every thing that began to exist (eg: all things material) has a cause for its existence which must lay outside itself.
4. The physical universe is a thing and thus also has a causal beginning.
5. Whatever is responsible for causing the universe to exist must be, by definition, immaterial, immensely powerful, and must transcend time/space (eternal/infinite).
6. We call this entity *God.*

Each of these premises has been well-defended by multiple theologians.[7,8]

---

7 For example, see William Lane Craig's defense of the Kalam Cosmological Argument here: https://www.reasonablefaith.org/writings/popular-writings/existence-nature-of-god/the-kalam-cosmological-argument?gad_source=1&gclid=CjwKCAiArLyuBhA7EiwA-qo80MSdFrnk4ERc8kkI1AguCsvtfXbq-RqWmxYktfbdtbsUfr3BuFKMCRoCTrUQAvD_BwE

8 For an accessible video on the subject, see the following: Part 1: https://www.youtube.com/watch?v=6CulBuMCLg0   Part 2: https://www.youtube.com/watch?v=vybNvc6mxMo

To summarize, we have not always been. Our nature *as well as* that of the universe is *contingent.* This means that our existence depends on something else. We were made by God, who Himself has *always* been. Remember that God's eternal nature is a necessary conclusion, not an assumption. The human mind may recoil at such a notion, and perhaps it is confusing to say that God has *always been* because it implies that He has always been *inside of time.*

This is, of course, impossible. We have already concluded that Time Itself has an origin with the Material Universe. Thus, God does not exist eternally *within* time. Rather, God *transcends* time. God simply *is.* Remarkably, this is how God speaking to Moses. In Exodus 3:14, God declared His name: "I AM THAT I AM (KJV)." In other words, He is the Eternally Present, Self-Existent One.

A Designer?

There is much more we can learn about God through observing the world around us. For example, the exquisite detail/order of nature describes to us a God who is an Artist and Architect. It is not as though this universe were haphazardly thrown together. Rather, a couple dozen fundamental forces and initial quantities (such as the strong/weak nuclear force or the initial amount of entropy) govern every physical interaction.[9] Think about this: It takes less constants to explain the universe than it does footnotes to explain this small booklet (if you include the biblical references). Marvelous simplicity and elegance, such as are observed in numbers like the Golden Ratio, Fibonacci's Number, and even $E=mc^2$, adorn the cosmos. Additionally, there are carefully calibrated relationships that are fantastically underappreciated. For example, consider the connection between the strength of Gravity compared to the value of the electromagnetic fine structure constant and the ratio of electron to proton mass. I know that sounds like a lot, and it is. But look at it anyway:

$$\alpha_G = 5.9 \times 10^{-39}$$

$$\alpha^{12}(m_e/m_p)^4 = 2.0 \times 10^{-39}$$

The first value is an extremely small number that represents the strength of Gravity. The second one is an extremely small number that represents a complex relationship of electromagnetism and the relative masses of electrons and protons. Notice how these two numbers are almost identical. Now, observe the exponents in the second number. If any of the independent variables were slightly different, the results would be massively different. What does it mean? Apparently, the fact that these values are so close to each other is what allows stars to form in just the right way. Here's what physicist Paul Davies said about this coincidence:

9 https://bigthink.com/starts-with-a-bang/how-many-constants-universe/

> The fact that the two sides of the inequality are such enormous numbers, and yet lie so close to one another, is truly astonishing. If gravity were very slightly weaker, or electromagnetism very slightly. stronger (or the electron slightly less massive relative to the proton) all stars would be red dwarfs. A correspondingly tiny change the other way, and they would all be blue giants.[10]

These startling cosmic alignments, along with the rest of creation, reveal to us a God who is both Intelligent and Intentional. Did you know that the most complex structure in the entire observable universe is the *human brain*? I don't know what's more amazing: The truth of that statement or the fact that we are aware of it. Yet, many mysteries of the universe remain, and may forever preclude our understanding. (Will there ever be an intelligible link that unifies Quantum Mechanics and General Relativity?) Who can say? These stunning realities point out a God who is Elusive and Infinite.

Up to this point, most of the population of the world will accept God in this way. After all, cosmologists and physicists articulate over and over again that Something immeasurably powerful and nonmaterial really is behind the whole universe.

10 P.C.W. Davies, THE ACCIDENTAL UNIVERSE (CUP, Cambridge, 1982), p.73

But if we stop here, we have an entity that has no *personage*. In other words, we might as well call this Reality a *FORCE*. This idea shows up in pop culture all the time such as in Star Wars, the MCU, and even with the concept of *Karma*. Let's look back at Romans 1:

> **Romans 1:18-23**
> *For God's wrath is revealed from heaven against all godlessness and unrighteousness of people who by their unrighteousness suppress the truth, since what can be known about God is evident among them, because God has shown it to them. For His invisible attributes, that is, His eternal power and divine nature, have been clearly seen since the creation of the world, being understood through what He has made. As a result, people are without excuse. **For though they knew God, they did not glorify Him as God or show gratitude.** Instead, their thinking became nonsense, and their senseless minds were darkened. Claiming to be wise, they became fools and exchanged the glory of the immortal God for images resembling mortal man, birds, four-footed animals, and*
> *reptiles.*

Notice the breakdown occurs when they don't want to glorify God *as God*. An atheist can accept a Powerful, Fundamental Force behind all reality *as long as* this force is not a Person. If the force is a Person, then, suddenly, I am accountable to this Person. I might have to say thank you and worship this Being.

Is God *Personal*?

At first, it might seem that assigning personhood to the Creator is merely *anthropomorphic* (giving human characteristics to non-humans) and, therefore, beneath Him. However, it is hard to imagine that the Ultimate Source of Time, Material, Life, Love, and Truth, is, somehow, both greater than us in all of these ways, and yet, less than us, when it comes to personhood. We take for granted the fact that something that does not possess personhood is less valuable in some respect. Do you feel bad when you step on a rock? What about a bacteria? In fact, some of the fierce philosophical debate on the topic of abortion has to do with when the living human in the womb inherits personhood (with the assumption being that non-persons are less valuable). As a side note, of course the living human in the womb is a person from conception, and worth protecting. Is God less than a person? On the contrary! God must be greater than us. If we, great as we are, and yet contingent beings, are *persons*, it naturally follows that God is at the very least a Divine Person, or perhaps more accurately, a SUPERPERSON(S). And if God is more than a *what*, if God is also a *who*, then we must acknowledge Him as He has revealed Himself to us.

Special Revelation

Hebrews 1:1-2a

Long ago God spoke to the fathers by the prophets at different times and in different ways. In these last days, He has spoken to us by His Son.

Special Revelation includes:

   a. The Word of God (scriptures)
   b. The Spirit of God

From studying the world and ourselves, we can conclude that God is the wonderous Eternal Creator of all that is. And, yet there is a second voice that cries out in the wilderness. It is sometimes referred to as *special revelation.* This is the unique, direct communication of the Divine to the man. Upon receiving this wisdom through the ministry of the Word of God and the Spirit of God, we discover that Nature and Reason are not liars. We have, as it were, confirmation of God's nature, established in the mouth of two or more witnesses. Additionally, we see in scripture specifically that God subsists as a Triune Being who comes to us as Father, Son, and Spirit. This *Trinity* is neither modalistic (one Divine Person in three modes) nor Tri-theistic (three distinct gods in agreement with each other). Rather, the scriptures reveal that God is One Being in Three Co-Equal, Co-Eternal Persons.

Created in His Image

Genesis 1:26-27

Then God said, "Let Us make man in Our image, according to Our likeness. They will rule the fish of the sea, the birds of the sky, the livestock, all the earth, and the creatures that crawl on the earth." So God created man in His own image; He created him in the image of God; He created them male and female.

This Triune Self-Existing One spoke in Genesis 1, *Let us make man in Our image.* What a startling thought! We are uniquely made in the image of God. What does this mean?

When we compare ourselves to the world around us, certain truths come into focus. Trees do not think. Fish do not care. Beasts show no compassion or mercy. They do not make moral choices. On the other hand, humans can reason, contemplate, create, love, sacrifice, worship, and appreciate what has been made. Humans have thoughts of eternity, desires for justice, longings for home, beauty, goodness, and truth.

Genesis 2:7
Then the Lord God formed the man out of the dust from the ground and breathed the breath of life into his nostrils, and the man became a living being.

Curiously, this is not said of any of the animal kingdom. God is the source of all life; and yet, human beings alone are capable of something more than our beastly friends. Here is one way to frame it: Notice in the figure that each form of life encompasses the awareness of the level beneath it while also going *beyond* it.

Basic life - awareness of environment

Plants are obviously alive in some sense. Flowers move toward the sunlight. Trees grow toward the water. However, there is a clear limit to their awareness.

Complex life - awareness of self

More complex animals can be said to have a soulish existence. By this, we mean that they are somewhat self-aware. A tree is aware of the environment but not aware of the distinction between itself and the environment. Conversely, dogs are aware of their environment, *and* they are aware that they are not the same thing as their environment. Dogs can also eat and play.

Human life - awareness of God

At the top of terrestrial life stands humanity ruling as kings and queens. Humans have a third level of awareness. They are aware of their environment, their selves in the environment, and they are aware of the One who made them and put them in the environment. Only human beings can know where they came from. There exists with that a certain nobility and freedom reminiscent of God. We can make choices that have moral implications. We are body, soul, and spirit. In this way, therefore, we are made in the image of God.

Now, it must be stated here that we are not the same as God. False religions will tempt vulnerable people with the notion that we are gods or can become gods. Nothing can be further from the truth. Imagine going into the restroom and looking at yourself in the mirror. It was designed to reflect the image of you back to you. It's very interesting to see infants see their reflection because they often confuse it with seeing another baby. However, as an adult, we know the difference. Though we are made to reflect God's glory and goodness, we dare not confuse this with actually being a god unto ourselves. This was, in fact, the original sin of Satan (Isaiah 14:12-15) and it was the temptation given to Eve in the garden:

> **Genesis 3:1-5**
> *"No! You will not die," the serpent said to the woman. "In fact, God knows that when you eat it your eyes will be opened and you will be like God, knowing good and evil."*

The implication is that she would no longer need God because she would be a god herself. This is a great error. There can be no greater distinction than the fact that God is the Eternal Uncreated Creator and we are temporal finite creatures. We are contingent beings while God is the Self-Existing One. Or, to put it another way, God is God and man is made to worship Him.

Back to **Genesis 1:27.** This thought concludes with stating that God made man, male and female. At first, this might seem confusing. However, man in Hebrew is referring to *mankind* or *humanity* (as opposed to animal kind or plant kind, not man as opposed to woman). So, God made human beings male and female. Notice the clarity. They are simply male and female. They are made complementary to one another. They both fully embody the stamp of God's image. They are distinct from each other and binary. Today, humanity still exists as male and female. Then, what about the gender spectrum and all of the LGBT rights? Where did it come from?

Much of what society believes today is the product of believing the lie about man's origin. Consider the implication of the words of renown Historian of Evolutional Biology, William Provine:

> Let me summarize my views on what modern evolutionary biology tells us loud and clear — and these are basically Darwin's views. There are no gods, no purposes, and no goal-directed forces of any kind. There is no life after death. When I die, I am absolutely certain that I am going to be dead. That's the end of me. There is no ultimate foundation for ethics, no ultimate meaning in life, and no free will for humans, either.[11]

11 Provine, W. 1994 Debate with Phil Johnson. (http://www.arn.org/docs/orpages/or161/

161main.htm)

Provine suggests that there is no ethical standard or moral imperative because 'there are no gods, no purposes'. In other words, he has rejected the truth that we are made *by* God and *for* God. Thus, the truth of our identity, origin, purpose, and destiny, is now called into question. With this paradigm, societies can make up their own values and distort the stamp of God's image. This is how civilizations unravel. Compare this type of thinking with the words of Jesus. When someone asked Him a question about divorce, notice His response:

> **Matt 19:3-8**
>
> *Some Pharisees approached Him to test Him. They asked, "Is it lawful for a man to divorce his wife on any grounds?" "Haven't you read," He replied, "that He who created them in the beginning made them male and female," and He also said: "For this reason a man will leave his father and mother and be joined to his wife, and the two will become one flesh? So they are no longer two, but one flesh. Therefore, what God has joined together, man must not separate."*
>
> *"Why then," they asked Him, "did Moses command us to give divorce papers and to send her away?"*
>
> *He told them, "Moses permitted you to divorce your wives because of the hardness of your hearts. But it was not like that from the beginning."*

Here, when addressing a contemporary cultural question about divorce, Jesus used Genesis 1-2 to ground a proper worldview. In other words, He didn't say 'well the Old Testament is totally irrelevant here. What we need to look at is what modern man is saying.' No, Jesus explained that the answer to the current question was found in the opening pages of the Bible. So, how do we address similar questions in our day and context? If we are following Jesus, we go back to the beginning. It's a question of our origin. This very simple observation demonstrates the danger of changing our beliefs of origin to conform to modern opinion.

What some things about our origin that you have learned that do not align with the Bible? How do you reconcile these?

How might Jesus address modern cultural controversies, such as abortion or LGBT rights?

Consider this summary of the secular origin story:

[meaninglessness->molecules->man]

How has this paradigm shaped our understanding of human dignity, sacredness, or responsibility?

Worship is the marveling in and praising of the One true God. We are made to worship. In fact, if we do not worship God, we will worship something else. If we read a few more verses in Romans 1, notice what happens:

> **Romans 1:21-24**
> *Claiming to be wise, they became fools and exchanged the glory of the immortal God for images resembling mortal man, birds, four-footed animals, and reptiles. Therefore, God delivered them over in the cravings of their hearts to sexual impurity, so that their bodies were degraded among themselves. They exchanged the truth of God for a lie, and worshiped and served something created instead of the Creator, who is praised forever. Amen.*

You must determine that God will be the Object of your worship. This can manifest as singing, declaring, testifying, meditating, acknowledging, etc. Worship is the *response* of the regenerated heart to the revelation of God's glory. In the New Testament, there are multiple words that translate as *worship*, but to keep it simple for now, let's describe worship as the following:

1. We worship God when we see who HE is, and marvel. God is truly awful in the old sense of the word (Full

of Awe). Learning about God through study, prayer, and meditation can often generate a sense of awe.

2. This is to make exclamatory declarations about God. When you shout or sing "God, you are good! You are holy!" you are giving Him praise.

3. Submission/Serve. When you hear the word worship, chances are you think of singing or bowing down. Indeed, there is a sense in which we fall down prostrate before Him and accept His Divinity and Authority over our lives.

Remember that we cannot help but worship something. Many people worship things, other people, or themselves. And yet, Jesus responded to this temptation from the devil with the following command:

> **Matthew 4:8-10**
> *Again, the Devil took Him to a very high mountain and showed Him all the kingdoms of the world and their splendor. And he said to Him, "I will give You all these things if You will fall down and worship me." Then Jesus told him, "Go away, Satan! For it is written: Worship the Lord your God, and serve only Him."*

Let us therefore, praise *Him*! Attend church services with other believers regularly to help you cultivate this virtue.

3

PURPOSE: Why am I here?

For whoever wants to save his life will lose it,
but whoever loses his life because of Me will find it.
-Matthew 16:25

One of the most interesting and peculiar things that life uniquely demonstrates is the impulsive and stubborn will to survive. Life is precious in this way and clearly distinct from nonlife. Further still, *intelligent* life is even more impressive, with an obsession to discover or, perhaps, recover the purpose of existence. One thing we can clearly observe: Those who have denied God will stop at nothing to try and understand themselves while, at the same time, boldly asserting that God is not the answer. They certainly don't want us believing that. Here is an excerpt from a recent article from BigThink:

Does life on Earth have a purpose?

The lesson from life is simple: In Nature, creation and destruction dance together. But there is no choreographer. The randomness of life makes it even more extraordinary that it evolved to include a species capable of asking about its own origins.[12]

Notice the startling conclusion. First, these scientists believe *a priori* ("from the first") that there is no God. Therefore, they marvel at the idea that, from the meaningless and mindless universe, which itself came from nothing intelligent, conscious creatures emerged randomly that could reach the point of actually being able to understand the whole history of the mindless beginning! This truly is a *faith* of sorts. Sadly, this kind of faith is very destructive. Here is a thought experiment:

Suppose there was a mountain. And this mountain was so large that you could not see its peak. In fact, it had *no peak*. It just kept going up. At the *top* of the mountain, a handful of garbage was released, and it began to fall down the mountain. On the way down, the garbage picked up pieces of the mountain, and, slowly but surely, formed into something very different. Because the mountain is *so tall*, it took something like billions of years

12 https://bigthink.com/13-8/life-earth-purpose/

for this garbage to fall and change. Eventually, the resulting mass became *sentient*. It started to think and feel. More time went by until, at a certain point, the mass was intelligent enough to understand that it was falling down a mindless mountain without a peak.

More years passed and, the mass came to realize the origins of itself as a handful of lifeless garbage that was paradoxically *released* from the *top* of the mountain without a peak, yet not *intentionally*. Hopefully, you can see that, among many other problems with this, lies the enigma of trusting the rationale which leads to the dissolving of *reason itself*.

This scenario is so implausible that it is absurd. And yet, it is more believable than what it proposed about the very nature of human beings! There is no conceivable end to the creativity of people who *strive* to *understand* while at the same time, denying the plain reality of God and His Purpose for us. You can observe this phenomenon for yourself! Find some friends or teachers that do not believe in God and ask curiously 'how do you suppose the universe came into being, and what is the ultimate purpose?' Watch as energetic voices begin to compete for more creative and elaborate ideas. Concepts like 'Quantum fields', 'floating membranes', and 'beginningless oscillating universes', will inevitably join the conversation at some point. And, of course, aliens will likely make an appearance. Literally everything is on the table *except* a Holy and Good Creator God.

Destructive Faith

At first, the word *faith* sounds inherently religious. However, it simply means that the belief originates *outside* the purview of observation and rigorous inquiry. There are plenty of non-religious people who have a lot of faith in their philosophy of relativistic purpose and morality. Perhaps the best summary of this worldview can be encapsulated in the unsourced but well-known quote from Japanese martial artist, Morihei Ueshiba:

Morihei Ueshiba, 1939
photo in the public domain

THERE ARE MANY PATHS LEADING TO THE TOP OF
MOUNT FUJI, BUT ONLY ONE SUMMIT – LOVE

What could be wrong with this idea? It's compassionate, inclusive, pleasant, and it appeals to a basic intuition that everything will work out in the end. The only problem with this type of faith is that it is false. It runs completely against God and the truth. As a result, it leads to destruction.

> **Proverbs 14:12, 16:25**
> *There is a way that seems right to a man, but its end is the way to death*

On the other hand, Jesus taught very simply that there are only two real paths: one of them wide, and one of them narrow.

> **Matthew 7:13-14**
> *"Enter through the narrow gate. For the gate is wide and the road is broad that leads to destruction, and there are many who go through it. How narrow is the gate and difficult the road that leads to life, and few find it.*

The wide path does not discriminate. It welcomes all forms of rebellion. In fact, it pleads with you: *choose your own path. Do what you want, what you think is right or good.*

Compare the two images on the following page and the opposing worldviews they represent

Worldly Philosophy
*There are many
acceptable paths*

Jesus Teaching
*There is one path that
leads to life and one
that leads to death*

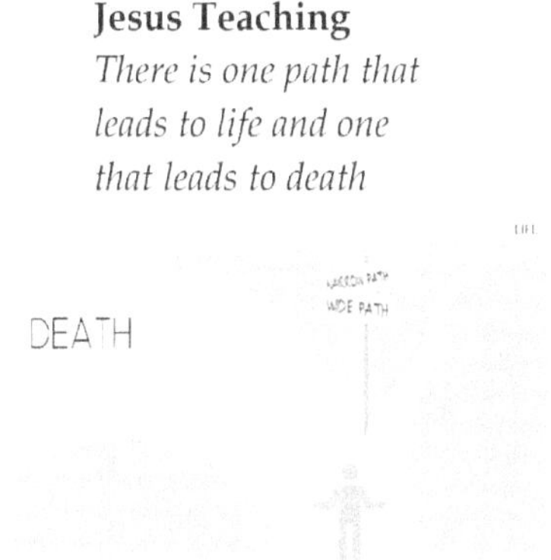

Jesus illustrates a stark and sobering proposition. It is either *turn to Him* or *fall to destruction*. There is no middle way and there are no *other* paths. This means that every way that presents itself as an alternative to Jesus, whether religious or secular, is still on the **broad road.** The broad road is *broad*. Myriads of people who think they are blazing their own trail or following a secret path to enlightenment will actually fall into destruction.

The god of this age

Who is the god of our culture? What may be startling to learn is that the answers you get on a survey and the answers you see in how people live are totally different. According to a recent Gallup poll, over 60% of Americans are "convinced that God exists."[13] This is the stronger choice of wording.

13 https://news.gallup.com/poll/268205/americans-believe-god.aspx

Many more Americans generally believe in God. But, even in the conservative case, the majority are convinced that a Just, Benevolent Creator is the real God. However, if you look at the way people live, you would think that the real gods are: money, treasure, pleasure, entertainment, status, etc. Jesus used a word to describe this. He called it MAMMON.

> **Matthew 6:24 KJV**
> *No man can serve two masters: for either he will hate the one, and love the other; or else he will hold to the one, and despise the other. Ye cannot serve God and* **mammon***.*

The Greek word is actually *mammōnâs,* and it is more than just money. Mammon is more like the evil influence of a materialistic, worldly confidence based on earthly wealth and security. In other words, mammon becomes a false god to which many are disposed to worship. Jesus said it plainly: We cannot worship God and worship Mammon. For the Christian, the purpose in life, therefore, cannot be ultimately reducible to a form of mammon worship. *So why am I here?*

I am going to share something with you that might appear strange or even shocking if you have never heard it, but it is true:

Your purpose in life is to *glorify* God.

Isaiah 43:6b-7
Bring My sons from far away,
and My daughters from the ends of the earth
*everyone called by My name and **created for My glory**.*
I have formed him; indeed, I have made him."

God made you to bring Him glory! *Wait a second,* someone says, *what does it mean to glorify God? and why does God care so much about His glory*? Before we address these questions, let's look back in the Old Testament to a story about Moses.

Moses, by all accounts, lived a unique life. He witnessed Divine deliverance on multiple occasions. God revealed Himself to Moses through many miracles. From the burning bush to the splitting of the Sea, Moses had encountered God's Glory over and over. And yet, after all this, Moses asks God for more.

Exodus 33:18
Then Moses said, "Please, let me see Your glory."

Here is the setting: The nation of Israel is being led by Moses through the wilderness like a disobedient child. There is idolatry, civil war, and a lot of sin. The people had witnessed a very impressive miracle at the base of Mount Sinai when God began to speak. But they couldn't handle it, so they sent Moses up. While he was gone, they decided it was more convenient to worship God as if He was a golden calf. They made up a version of God that was okay with their indulgent lifestyle. When Moses reappeared, he saw firsthand how easily led astray the human heart can be. After the fighting was over, Moses went up again, this time even more desperate for an encounter with God. It is here where we find this strange account of Moses asking to see God's Glory.

Exodus 33:18-23

Then Moses said, "Please, let me see Your glory." He said, "I will cause all My goodness to pass in front of you, and I will proclaim the name Yahweh before you. I will be gracious to whom I will be gracious, and I will have compassion on whom I will have compassion." But He answered, "You cannot see My face, for no one can see Me and live." The LORD said, "Here is a place near Me. You are to stand on the rock, and when My glory passes by, I will put you in the crevice of the rock and cover you with My hand until I have passed by. Then I will take My hand away, and you will see My back, but My face will not be seen."

The first question you might ask is, *hadn't Moses seen enough?* Surely, with everything that Moses had already seen of God, he should be content. However, it is almost like the more Moses sees God's glory, the more he wants to see God's glory. Moses is not the only one. Look at what these three other guys said:

David (Psalm 27:4)

*I have asked one thing from the LORD; **it is what I desire**: to dwell in the house of the LORD all the days of my life, **gazing on the beauty of the LORD** and seeking Him in His temple.*

Isaiah (Isaiah 26:8-9)

Yes, Yahweh, we wait for You in the path of Your judgments.
Our desire is for Your name and renown.
I long for You in the night;
*yes, my spirit within me **diligently seeks You**,*

Paul (Philippians 3:8)

More than that, I also consider everything to be a loss in view of the surpassing value of knowing Christ Jesus my Lord. Because of Him I have suffered the loss of all things and consider them filth, so that I may gain Christ,

Many testimonies exist in the scriptures of men and women who have seen something of God's Glory and, as a result, desire nothing more. What did they know that we haven't yet discovered? You might have heard some preacher once, saying that our sole purpose is to bring God glory, but it might have sounded cold or pointless. Even more importantly, it might have sounded like it's the opposite of what we want to do with our lives. So why do these people in the bible seem to want nothing more than His glory? Perhaps it will help if we ask a more basic question:

WHAT IS GOD'S GLORY?

The Glory of God

Glory, this word often repeated in the Bible, is often used in ambiguous ways, but it does have a meaning. In an interview with Desiring God, John Piper defines God's glory this way:

> ...the glory of God is the manifest beauty of his holiness.[14]

Let's break it down. In one sense, God is *unknowable*. This is sort of what holiness means. God is utterly unique and there is no other to compare to Him. Even though man is created in God's Image, there is an infinite distance between CREATOR and CREATED. Imagine for a moment that you drew a cartoon that could walk and talk. Even if this cartoon could *think*, there is obviously a sense in which he could never *know* you. The distance between you and the cartoon is immense! One would struggle to even measure it, but it is surely at least several orders of magnitude. As hard to fathom as that might be, compared to the distance between you and God, you and the cartoon would look like twins. His Perfections of Love, Truth, Joy, Beauty, Justice, are all equally immeasurable. So how does anyone *know* God? It is through His Glory. In other words, when the holiness (otherness) of God becomes manifest, it is described as *Glory*, and it is weighty and breath-taking.

14 https://www.desiringgod.org/interviews/what-is-gods-glory--2

Psalm 19:1-2
The heavens declare the glory of God, and the sky proclaims the work of His hands. Day after day they pour out speech; night after night they communicate knowledge.

Here's another wat to describe it. The Glory of God is the solidness or REAL-NESS of His Nature breaking into the physical realm. It is both alarming and alluring. To be sure, it is a *good* thing. The angels in heaven, being free from the stain of sin, can bask in God's presence and enjoy His Glory forever. For sinful man, however, there is a big problem.

When the prophet Isaiah gets a glimpse of God, his first reaction is to cry out, **"Woe is me! for I am undone; because I am a man of unclean lips"** (Isaiah 6:5 KJV). Sin has a way of turning a man into a shadow, and what could be more frightening than for a shadow to meet light? Enter the power of the gospel. In Christ, God takes a dead shadow of a man, and makes him come alive!

2 Corinthians 5:17
Therefore, if anyone is in Christ, he is a new creation; old things have passed away, and look, new things have come.

Therefore, to the redeemed soul, **seeing more of God's Glory, or *glorifying God*, becomes the central longing of his heart and the purpose of his life.**

It is important to understand that when you *glorify God*, you are simply participating in the breaking forth of God's wonderous elusive beauty into our world. We not only desire this for ourselves, but we understand that God's Glory is the best thing for all creation. If "Every generous act and every perfect gift is from above, coming down from the Father of lights" (James 1: 17), then the best gift that God can give anyone is *Himself*.

How does He give someone Himself? Especially considering that He is Holy, how can the Infinite, *unknowable* God, connect with the finite creature? The answer is: through His Glory. Through His glory, the color of flowers becomes *color*. Through His glory, the taste of fresh water becomes *water*. Through the manifest beauty of His holiness (His Glory), God awakens the soul to *Zoë*. Remember that Zoë is the transcendent eternal life which enables us to become Sons of God. When the soul is made alive to God, the notion that all good things are really reflections of Him surpasses the level of mere poetry. Like the old psalmist says:

> *Psalm 34:8a*
> *Taste and see that the LORD is good.*

To be sure, this gift of life is only possible because of the death and resurrection of the Christ, and it can only be received though faith in Him (see chapter 1).

I have often wondered, *why would not every man receive this gospel gladly*? There is, of course, a real resistance to the eternal life (*Zoë*) offered by Christ. In *Mere Christianity*, C. S. Lewis writes about the extent of the transformation and the peculiar resistance to it:

The natural life in each of us is something self-centered, something that wants to be petted and admired, to take advantage of other lives, to exploit the whole universe. And especially it wants to be left to itself: to keep well away from anything better or stronger or higher than it, anything that might make it feel small. It is afraid of the light and air of the spiritual world, just as people who have been brought up to be dirty are afraid of a bath. And in a sense it is quite right. It knows that if the spiritual life gets hold of it, all its self-centeredness and self-will are going to be killed and it is ready to fight tooth and nail to avoid that. Did you ever think, when you were a child, what fun it would be if your toys could come to life? Well suppose you could really have brought them to life. Imagine turning a tin soldier into a real little man. It would involve turning the tin into flesh. And suppose the tin soldier did not like it. He is not interested in flesh; all he sees is that the tin is being spoilt. He thinks you are killing him. He will do everything he can to prevent you. He will not be made into a man if he can help it.[15]

15 C.S. Lewis, *Mere Christianity*, "The Obstinate Toy Soldiers" 1952, p. 178-179

For the Christian, the answer to the question before us (*Why am I here?*) is simple: We exist to bring God Glory, and that is a good thing!

Let's say for a moment you could sit down with Paul or Peter or Moses or Elijah or David, or many other individuals from times past, and you could ask them this question: "What is the good life?"

With one voice, they would all respond, "To God be the Glory!" To put it another way, listen to the shout of those souls in Revelation 5 who are basking in God's Presence:

> **Revelation 5:13-14**
> *I heard every creature in heaven, on earth, under the earth,*
> *on the sea, and everything in them say:*
> *Blessing and honor and glory and dominion*
> *to the One seated on the throne,*
> *and to the Lamb, forever and ever!*
> *The four living creatures said, "Amen,"*
> *and the elders fell down and worshipped.*

Now there yet remains one important question on this topic:

HOW DO WE BRING GOD
GLORY?

How to Glorify God

That is, how do we usher in more of God's beauty to this place? For this brief exploration, we shall reduce the answer to three simple observations:

1. We glorify God through FAITH by *believing Him at His Word*
2. We glorify God through WORSHIP by giving Him *praise*
3. We glorify God through WORKS by letting *His light shine through us* to others

Remember that, in all of these observations, the central aspiration is to turn the gaze toward God. If what you do draws attention to yourself *instead* of God, then it is false.

I. Believe Him

We glorify God in displaying our belief in what He has revealed.

When a Christian believes God, this results in *inward trust* and *outward obedience*. When you trust God, your inner self beholds His Glory. It is almost as if God comes closer and closer into focus as you are drawn toward Him. As you trust Him today, you are given more strength to trust Him tomorrow. Notice how David demonstrated this faith right before he went to kill Goliath:

1 Samuel 17:31-37

What David said was overheard and reported to Saul, so he had David brought to him. David said to Saul, "Don't let anyone be discouraged by him; your servant will go and fight this Philistine!" But Saul replied, "You can't go fight this Philistine. You're just a youth, and he's been a warrior since he was young."

*David answered Saul: "Your servant has been tending his father's sheep. Whenever a lion or a bear came and carried off a lamb from the flock, I went after it, struck it down, and rescued the lamb from its mouth. If it reared up against me, I would grab it by its fur, strike it down, and kill it. Your servant has killed lions and bears; this uncircumcised Philistine will be like one of them, for he has defied the armies of the living God." **Then David said, "The Lord who rescued me from the paw of the lion and the paw of the bear will rescue me from the hand of this Philistine."** Saul said to David, "Go, and may the Lord be with you."*

David credited his victory over the wild animals to God's protection. In other words, the confidence that David displayed was really a reflection of his faith in God. The word *confidence* comes from Latin which means "with faith" (*con-fidere*). The faith that David demonstrated brought glory to God by directing all the focus upward, which in turn, encouraged David to trust God even more. Finally, when David actually (spoiler alert) defeated Goliath, Israel recognized that the victory was due to God and not to David.

You can bring God glory by directing your heart toward Him in faith. There are many Christians who come this far, and then, something gets lost. They want to *believe* God, but they do not want to *obey* Him. Notice, however, that if you believe God when He tells you to do something, it will lead to your obedience. Or, to put it negatively:

> **Luke 6:46**
> [Jesus] *Why do you call Me 'Lord, Lord,' and don't do the things I say?*

According to Jesus, the Christian cannot abide in *belief* while remaining in *disobedience*.

You might have heard that God is not so much interested in how you obey His commands, just as long as you accept the gift that Jesus has offered in the cross. Compare this thought with the following verse:

> **Ephesians 2:8-10**
> *For you are saved by grace through faith, and this is not from yourselves; it is God's gift not from works, so that no one can boast. For we are His creation, created in Christ Jesus for good works, which God prepared ahead of time so that we should walk in them.*

While you cannot depend on your obedience to *merit* eternal life, you should understand that once you are brought into God's family through faith, your faith will lead to a desire and capability to follow His commands.

What are His commands?

1 John 5:3
For this is what love for God is: to keep His commands. Now His commands are not a burden.

Following Jesus means to abide in Him and, therefore, it is not as simple checking off a list of rules. However, let us examine just two of these commands given to Christians:

1. **Believers' Baptism**

Matthew 28:18-20
*Then Jesus came near and said to them, "All authority has been given to Me in heaven and on earth. Go, therefore, and make disciples of all nations, **baptizing them** in the name of the Father and of the Son and of the Holy Spirit, teaching them to observe everything I have commanded you. And remember, I am with you always, to the end of the age."*

One of the easiest commands for Christians in the New Testament is to publicly display your faith in Christ by water baptism. The water doesn't *regenerate* your heart, but it does *reveal* your faith. Christians are never called to a hide their faith under a basket (Matt. 5:15-16). Remember that **faith is personal but not private.**

Have you been baptized in water as a believer in Christ?

2. Honoring God in your Body

1 Corinthians 6:18-20

Run from sexual immorality! "Every sin a person can commit is outside the body." On the contrary, the person who is sexually immoral sins against his own body. Don't you know that your body is a sanctuary of the Holy Spirit who is in you, whom you have from God? You are not your own, for you were bought at a price. Therefore, glorify God in your body.

Notice, Paul gives two reasons that we are to honor God with our bodies.

1. We are temples of the Holy Spirit
2. We are purchased by Christ with blood

The idea of honoring God with your body is something that is mostly lost in our pluralistic society. Christians in American culture have been heavily influenced by gnostic dualism which subtly teaches that God saves the soul but not the body. "Therefore, do whatever you will with the flesh!" This cannot be true, for **Christ rose in the body!** The Cosmic Plan of Redemption includes the rescue of the body, soul, and spirit. The entrance of the Holy Spirit into our bodies becomes the seal and promise of this future glorification. This means that, even now, we become temples of God's Holy Spirit! His Presence is with and in the

Christian. Still, many Christians live as though their bodies are meant to be used and abused. Consider the following sins and how they might diminish the glory of God:

Addictions and gluttonous appetites – **Phil 3:19**
Mutilation of the flesh - **Phil 3:2**
Fornication and sexual perversion – **Gal. 5:16-24**
Slothfulness and vanity – **Matt. 25:26**

What are you doing now that denigrates your body?
How does this behavior display our unbelief?

Remember that we first glorify God through Faith. Believing God at His Word produces both *inward trust* and *outward obedience*. With that, let us now move to the second way that we can glorify God.

II. Praise Him

We glorify God through our wonder and worship.

> Luke 2:13-14
> *Suddenly there was a multitude of the heavenly host with the angel, praising God and saying: Glory to God in the highest heaven, and peace on earth to people He favors!*

One of the best ways to bring glory to God is to exclaim the wonders of His Nature. Sometimes all you can do is shout

Glory! Do you remember walking out of the movie theater after seeing a life-changing film? What did you do afterward? Did you find it difficult to remain quiet? Probably, like most people, you immediately started messaging your friends about how good the movie was. You extolled the beauty and wonder of the film itself and the impact it had on you. This is somewhat similar to what happens when a Christian praises God.

Praise is in our DNA. We necessarily praise what moves us. Imagine hearing a really good joke and never being allowed to share it. What a tragedy! Here's another helpful quote from Lewis:

> I think we delight to praise what we enjoy because the praise not merely expresses but completes the enjoyment; it is its appointed consummation. It is not out of compliment that lovers keep on telling one another how beautiful they are; the delight is incomplete till it is expressed. It is frustrating to have discovered a new author and not to be able to tell anyone how good he is; to come suddenly, at the turn of the road, upon some mountain valley of unexpected grandeur and then to have to keep silent because the people with you care for it no more than for a tin can in the ditch; to hear a good joke and find no one to share it with[16]

16 essay titled, "A Word About Praising," in his short book, Reflections on the Psalms, pgs. 90–98

Lewis correctly pointed out that praising what we enjoy is more than *expressing* the enjoyment. It is the *completion of the enjoyment*. This means we cannot fully enjoy God *unless* we are praising Him. What a marvelous thought! It is no wonder that the command to praise God echoes through the corridors of scripture, Old and New Testament. How might this revelation change the way you sing next Sunday with your church?

> **Eph 3:20-21**
> *Now to him who is able to do far more abundantly than all that we ask or think, according to the power at work within us, to him be glory in the church and in Christ Jesus throughout all generations, forever and ever. Amen.*

> **Revelation 4:11**
> *"Worthy are you, our Lord and God, to receive glory and honor and power, for you created all things, and by your will they existed and were created."*

Do you find it difficult to sing or shout about the glory of God?

What reasons might make singing about a football team easier than singing about God?

What are some things you can praise God for today?

In conclusion, let us consider this simple outline:

1.   *We praise what we love/enjoy.*
2.   *Praise increases/completes that joy.*
3.   *We love/enjoy God.*
4.   *Praising God brings God Glory.*
5.   *We live to glorify God.*

Therefore, we will praise God because we love Him and because we live to bring Him Glory.

So far, we have considered two ways we can glorify God. We glorify God through faith in believing and obeying Him, and we glorify Him through worship in our praise. We will now look at one more example of how we can bring God glory.

III. Serve Him

In one sense, believing God will produce a desire to obey His commands. Yet, there is something more to say about bringing the light of God to others. We glorify God, that is, we bring His invisible beauty into focus, when others witness the light of God in us.

Matthew 5:16

In the same way, let your light shine before others, so that they may see your good works and give glory to your Father who is in heaven.

From the moment that a Christian begins his journey following Christ, he discovers that this is a public pursuit. He cannot follow Christ *privately*. This is evident in the very nature of what it means to follow Jesus. Notice how Jesus words it to His first disciples: "Follow Me," Jesus told them, "and I will make you fish for people!" (Matt. 4:19)

To be a Christian means to share the heart that Jesus has. What does Jesus value? The answer is clear from His ministry. Jesus wants *people*. Consider all of the things He could have said that day. He could have said, "Follow Me, and I will make you true worshippers" or "Follow Me, and I will make you believers of truth". Of course, we believe that following Jesus includes believing truth and worshipping God. However, Jesus said, "Follow Me, and I will make you fish for people." Considering the priority put on people, you must ask yourself this question:

If I am not fishing for people, am I really following Jesus?

Before we progress, we must now address two things:

1. What is the difference between salvation *by* works and the response of a Christian to the work of God?
2. What does it mean to *fish for people?*

Let us start with a potential misconception. Some people may confuse the *consequence* of salvation with the *requirements* of salvation. There are no *works* that you can do to earn the salvation of God. The gift of eternal life (Zoë) is a gift! This gift was purchased with the blood of the Savior Himself, and therefore, there is none that can afford it. The only way we can experience the gift is by *receiving it* from God. This is called Grace. And if Grace is by works, then grace is no more grace (Romans 11:6). Alas! Salvation is *by* Grace *through* faith (Eph. 2:8). Now, this Grace is not of no effect. On the contrary, when a person becomes a genuine believer, the heart is converted! What was dead spiritually is now made alive.

> **Ephesians 5:13-14**
> *Everything exposed by the light is made clear, for what makes everything clear is light. Therefore, it is said:*
> *Get up, sleeper, and rise up from the dead, and the Messiah will shine on you.*

Many passages such as this detail the transformation that takes place in the heart of the believer now regenerated. Because of this, there is a distinct growing in our faith, love, and obedience. This is what Paul calls the *fruit of the Spirit* (Galatians 5:22). It is a work of God in the believer. Therefore, serving God is not what makes us saved, but it is evidence that we are.

The second question presented asks 'what does it mean to fish for people?' The answer may be more than you think.

To begin, we must acknowledge that fishing for people must include *declaring the gospel to the unbelieving world*. This may manifest as sharing our testimony, such as is the case with the healed demoniac (Mark 5:1-20). The story ends with Jesus telling him:

Mark 5:19-20

He told him, "Go back home to your own people, and report to them how much the Lord has done for you and how He has had mercy on you." So he went out and began to proclaim in the Decapolis how much Jesus had done for him, and they were all amazed.

Fishing for people also includes preaching the gospel in the pulpit, on the streets, in the neighborhood, on campus, and across the world. Fishing for people includes planting churches around the country and beyond. We can, perhaps, refer to all of this as *direct evangelism.* But, we must be careful to observe this simple truth: The purpose for evangelism is to **bring glory to God**. It is not a competition or a campaign of man. It is the response of the regenerate heart making much of the name of Jesus. Evangelism is not an end unto itself. Rather, it is one lane in a mega highway of glorifying God. It is also important to observe that 'fishing for people' includes more than directly speaking about Jesus. It demonstrates a total paradigm shift.

Matthew 5:16

In the same way, let your light shine before others, so that they may see your good works and give glory to your Father who is in heaven.

Christians live in the light of God's truth. Everything we do now is oriented, though imperfectly, in such a way as to direct others to God.

Titus 3:8

This saying is trustworthy. I want you to insist on these things, so that those who have believed God might be careful to devote themselves to good works. These are good and profitable for everyone

For example, let's say that you entered college as a vaguely religious person with a set major of, say, *business*. You thought your mission in life was to own your own business and work on engineering projects. While in school, someone approached you with the gospel of Jesus Christ, and you became a strong believer. Now, how do you bring glory to God? Here is one possible answer: You continue your degree focus, and after graduating, you get an opportunity to start a business, travel to the poor regions in Mexico and use your skills to set up access to clean water. Eventually, your efforts evolve into a global ministry serving millions. When asked why you are doing this, you say something like, 'I want to glorify God in my life. Through serving these people in need, I can allow Jesus to shine His light through me.' You partner with missionaries to bring the truth of the gospel to those in need. Your ministry is called, say, "Lifewater." If that sounds too far-fetched, let me introduce you to Bill Ashe, the actual founder of Lifewater International. Bill died in 2016, having dedicated his life to living as a disciple of Jesus. His story can become your story.[17] There are thousands of people like Bill, who want to glorify God in their lives.

Of course, there are also folks who have sought to live in service to others but without all the baggage of *glorifying God*. A skeptic might inquire, *Why do I have to always give God the credit?*

To this objection, we must realize that the unbelieving world will not understand that *all* good things, whether great or small, are derived from God's goodness. The world will perhaps also not understand that good deeds, *in and of themselves*, are not the end. Rather, they are arrows pointing us to the true end, God Himself. There is no such thing as good apart from God. In either case, I am not speaking about this to the unbelieving world. I am speaking to you.

> **1 Cor 10:31**
> *Therefore, whether you eat or drink, or whatever you do, do everything for God's glory.*

To summarize, the follower of Jesus has discovered the central purpose of life is to bring glory to God. Glory is the manifestation of God's holiness. As God's glory expands, so too does the joy of man. We can glorify Him through *faith, worship,* and *service.*

---

17 *To learn more about Lifewater, visit: https://lifewater.org/blog/christian-non-profit-organization-anniversary/*

With these things in mind, we agree with the ancient Christian cry,

SOLI DEO GLORIA! (*To God alone be the Glory*)

How does your current environment present challenges to believing God?

When is the last time you felt like giving God some praise? Why is it sometimes more/less difficult?

What are some ways that you can serve God today? at school? at your job/home?

Do you have friends that are not Christians? How can you direct them closer to God?

What are some other ways you can glorify God in all things?

By study, we are referring specifically to the study of God's Word. For clarity, in this place, God's Word will be used interchangeably with the Bible (Old Testament and New Testament). As a student, you will spend much time studying subjects related to your major. However, as a Christian, the most important study you will engage in is the study of the scriptures. We can begin to know God by observing the things that He has revealed to us. Many biblical scholars have remarked that even after 50+ years of study, they have yet to exhaust the depth of the knowledge and understanding in the Bible. It is the most important book of all time. Nearly the wisest man who ever lived, Solomon is credited with the following proverbs:

> **Proverbs 2:1-6**
> *My son, if you accept my words and store up my commands within you, listening closely to wisdom and directing your heart to understanding; furthermore, if you call out to insight and lift your voice to understanding, if you seek it like silver and search for it like hidden treasure, then you will understand the fear of the Lord and discover the knowledge of God. For the Lord gives wisdom; from His mouth come knowledge and understanding.*

Proverbs 3:13-15

Happy is a man who finds wisdom and who acquires understanding, for she is more profitable than silver, and her revenue is better than gold. She is more precious than jewels; nothing you desire compares with her.

Proverbs 4:7

Wisdom is supreme—so get wisdom. And whatever else you get, get understanding.

Proverbs 16:16

Get wisdom—how much better it is than gold! And get understanding—it is preferable to silver.

In our current world of YouTube and TickTock, we have been conditioned to seek the visual SparkNotes of wisdom. We are satisfied with hearing the revelation that others have received. However, nothing can replace your own personal reading and studying of the bible itself. Carve out some time in your daily schedule to learn more about God through His Word! If you do not know where to begin, start with one of the four gospels (Matthew, Mark, Luke, John) and **read it all the way through**. Write down every question that comes into your mind and share these with your mentor. Now, I'm going to share something that jettisoned me forward into reading the bible for myself: Find a checklist (that includes chapters), like this one*, and mark your progress (and thank me later)!

*https://static1.squarespace.com/static/5d4c2acd65e8a5000190bc6f/t/5e020ebe6c5ca6277766bb68/1577193151638/bibrdgck.pdf

4

DESTINY: Where am I going?

*Your heart must not be troubled. Believe in God; believe also in
Me. In My Father's house are many dwelling places; if not, I
would have told you. I am going away to prepare a place for you.
If I go away and prepare a place for you, I will come back and
receive you to Myself, so that where I am you may be also*

John 14:1-3

You remember the never-ending struggle as a kid stuck in the
backseat of a car? Always confused about the details of a trip,
when, suddenly, you became a philosopher and start asking this
profound question: WHERE ARE WE GOING?

Now imagine one day that, after you ask this question, your
parent looks back at you and says: 'well we are going to a sea of
nothingness and then drive for about 20 miles and then just crash
into the ditch of darkness and despair, and then, explode.' Well,
that would be horrifying. And, even more importantly, it would

not truly answer the question. To say that you are going to no *where* and to no *thing*, is to say that you are not *really* going.

"Where are we going?"
"We're not."

Surely you can understand how deeply unsatisfying this answer is, and yet it is this tiresome answer we hear over and over when it comes to our ultimate destiny. Consider the following quotes from two of the most famous scientists of the 20th century:

Stephen Hawking in the 1980s
Photo taken by NASA, public domain

I regard the brain as a computer which will stop working when its components fail. There is no heaven or afterlife for broken down computers; that is a fairy story for people afraid of the dark.[18]

18 Hawking, Steven. Interview with the Guardian: https://www.theguardian.com/science/ 2011/may/15/stephen-hawking-interview-there-is-no-heaven

> " I would love to believe that when I die, I will live again, that some thinking, feeling, remembering part of me will continue. But as much as I want to believe that, and despite the ancient and worldwide cultural traditions that assert an afterlife, I know of nothing to suggest that it is more than wishful thinking[19] "

Carl Sagan in 1970s
Taken by NASA, public domain

Is there life after death?

For the typical person in today's society, this life is viewed as all there is. Religion is, of course, allowed in our culture, but throughout your entire public education and socialization, you are told to believe a little secret: *It's ok to go to church and read the bible, but we all know that it's not actually true. Nothing really happens after you die.* And yet, despite the constant echoing of this mantra, something internal witnesses to us that there must be something more.

---

19 Sagan, Carl. Billions & Billions: Thoughts on Life and Death at the Brink of the Millennium

There is a destination for man. He is bound to his Maker.

> **Hebrews 9:27-28**
> *And just as it is appointed for people to die once—and after this, judgment—so also the Messiah, having been offered once to bear the sins of many, will appear a second time, not to bear sin, but to bring salvation to those who are waiting for Him.*

So, what will happen after this life ends? The answer in the scripture is that we will all stand before God and give an account for our lives. Perhaps you can hear someone say, *maybe there is something or maybe not. Either way, why does it matter?* They go one to tell us that we should simply live as though this is the only life we have. Just, you know, embrace every moment!

That's a great idea when it comes to taking a picnic at the beach with your family, but when there are substantial challenges, it is good to understand how the nature of the eternal life adds to the depth of *this* life. One of the most dramatic realities that we experience in this life is the problem of suffering. In the worst case, a man perpetrates some horrific evil on numerous people and then kills himself or dies before being brought to justice. It feels almost like he escaped. What do the families of the victims do with this great injustice? There are only two options available. According to the law of the excluded middle[20], there can be no third alternative. Whether we like it or not, one, and only one, of the following propositions must be true.

Two Possibilities

1. Final justice is an illusion. The permanent wrongs committed will never *actually* be made right. In fact, right/wrong are, themselves, illusions.
2. There will be a day of reckoning when all is made right. The criminal will face the Eternal Judge.

The first option is the only one that the world can truly offer. Under this view, we are permitted, of course, to believe in some *temporal* or *proximate* justice. However, we are forced to accept that REAL justice, in the cosmic sense, is illusory. The problem here is obvious. If *real* justice is false, what is *proximate* justice, other than pure vengeance? Every time we experience an injustice, we cry out 'That's not fair!' When we assert the insurrection of this imbalance, we project an inner intuition that there is such a thing as *fair*. Real justice is simply bringing moral equality to the universe. If we live under the first option (given by the world), we will actually suffer more and feel a sense of disconnect with ourselves and with reality. This disconnect extends beyond justice. It also touches love, beauty, and truth itself. Nothing remains, except pure will and circumstance.

20 Not to be confused with the *fallacy* of the excluded middle, the law of excluded middle states that a proposition is true or its negation is true. Thus, eternal cosmic Justice is true or it is an illusion. There is no middle ground.

Conversely, knowing that there is a judgment after this life, offers a greater and more *real* love, joy, peace. We find that we are more connected with ourselves and the environment. We can say 'Justice is real! Love is real! Truth is real!' The difference between these two worldviews cannot be overstated. In one, we experience falling further into a dream where every solid boundary eventually gives way. In the other, we find ourselves truly *awake*. We can face many trials with courage knowing that this is not the end.

What happens at the judgment?

The Last Day

> *2 Corinthians 5:10-11*
> *For we must all appear before the tribunal (judgment) of Christ, so that each may be repaid for what he has done in the body, whether good or worthless. Therefore, because we know the fear of the Lord, we seek to persuade people. We are completely open before God, and I hope we are completely open to your consciences as well*

> *Revelation 20:11-15*
> *Then I saw a great white throne and One seated on it. Earth and heaven fled from His presence, and no place was found for them. I also saw the dead, the great and the small, standing before the throne, and books were opened. Another book was opened, which is the book of life, and the dead were judged according to their works by what was written in the books. Then the sea gave up its dead, and Death and*

Hades gave up their dead; all[f] were judged according to their works. Death and Hades were thrown into the lake of fire. This is the second death, the lake of fire. And anyone not found written in the book of life was thrown into the lake of fire.

From these verses, it is clear that this judgment will be like no other. Every soul from every time will stand alone before the Creator, and all that has been done is recorded. Some might read this and conclude that God will bring us to Heaven or send us to Hell *according* to *our works*. However, this is not what the text says. The only consideration for entrance into the Holy City is whether or not the person's name is written in the **book of life**. This book is referenced a few times in the Bible. Here are a couple of them:

Luke 10:19-20

Look, I have given you the authority to trample on snakes and scorpions and over all the power of the enemy; nothing will ever harm you. However, don't rejoice that the spirits submit to you, but rejoice that your names are written in heaven.

Revelation 21:27

(speaking of the New Heavenly Jerusalem) Nothing profane will ever enter it: no one who does what is vile or false, but only those written in the Lamb's book of life.

So what are these *other* books?

From the context of these passages, we can see that those whose names are not written in the book of life are judged *according to their works*. None of their works will save them, but this judgment is still critical because God is JUST. The punishment, though eternal, will match the works of the individual. For more on the nature of God's just treatment of the sinner, see James 3:1, Luke 12:41-48.

The point is that *no one* will be cast into the lake of fire without first being judged. Thus, they will have no excuse.

On the other hand, whosoever has his name in the Lamb's Book of Life will be saved. Yet, he will still stand before Christ and give an account. This is spoken in more detail in Paul's first letter to the church at Corinth:

> **1 Corinthians 3:11-15**
> *For no one can lay any other foundation than what has been laid down. That foundation is Jesus Christ. If anyone builds on that foundation with gold, silver, costly stones, wood, hay, or straw, each one's work will become obvious, for the day will disclose it, because it will be revealed by fire; the fire will test the quality of each one's work. If anyone's work that he has built survives, he will receive a reward. If anyone's work is burned up, it will be lost, but he will be saved; yet it will be like an escape through fire.*

Believers will be judged on the basis of their works to receive rewards, not to receive eternal life. No one man can merit eternal life by their own works, except the Man, Jesus Christ. That is why we receive His Righteousness as a covering over us, while our guilt is transferred to the cross (2 Cor. 5:21).

Many religions, and indeed our own intuition, instructs us to try to compensate for the wrongs we have committed (restitution). On the one hand, restitution is good and important. For example, if you crash into another car, you should compensate the owner with payment. However, if we take this idea and start to believe that we can compensate God, we lose the entire point of the gospel. He died *for us* precisely because we cannot pay for our own sin. Imagine this scenario:

You go to a party and participate in foolish behavior resulting in your complete inebriation. You stumble into your car and try to drive home. In the process, you unintentionally yet recklessly smashed into another driver. As you get out of the car, you observe that you have caused *permanent* damage to one of the passengers in the other vehicle. What can you do? Of course, you want to help as much as possible. You will apologize over and over. You bring gifts to their family and pay them visits. You pledge your allegiance to never drink again. However, there really is nothing that you can do to actually compensate them for the harm you have caused. They will likely receive your gifts because you both know that these gestures of good will are not *actual* payment for the crimes, but rather, a symbol of your compassion, concern and remorse. If you showed up one day to their house and gave them a check for a thousand dollars and said 'well, that should fully compensate you for the evil I've done. So, we're even now right?'

This would be extremely insulting, and the family would probably refuse your check because of what you think the check is. Your false understanding has the effect of degrading the value of the other persons life and well being. This will create more friction and distance. It can be no less with the Creator of the universe. When we sin, we mar the stamp of God's image, we insult the Divine Dignity, and we rebel against a Holy God. There is nothing we can do that will *truly* pay for this cosmic crime. Additionally, even our best attempts to do so, are tainted with sin. For real reconciliation and forgiveness, there must be a sufficient payment. This was foreshadowed in the garden of Eden when Adam and his wife disobeyed the command of God. In response to their crime, they tried to hide and make clothing out of fig leaves. When God showed up, He condemned their sin and false covering, but He did not leave them naked in their shame:

> **Genesis 3:21**
> *The Lord God made clothing out of skins for Adam and his wife, and He clothed them.*

To conclude, for real Divine compensation, we cannot offer our own works but we can decide whether or not to receive the work that has been given for us. The Perfect sacrifice of Christ was sufficient to *truly* cover our sin and shame. Today, if we pretend that we can pacify God's Holy Wrath on our own, we add insult to injury, and trample over the blood of Christ. Receiving the gift of eternal life by surrendering to Him in faith, is synonymous with having our names written in the Lamb's Book of Life. Rejoice therefore! Jesus says to rejoice that your name is written in heaven, for it means not only that you have been forgiven, but also that you belong to Him and will enter in to that CITY! (For more on this Judgement, see: Luke 13:22-30, Matt. 7:13-23, Matt. 25:31-46)

What happens *after* the judgment?

The New City

Revelation 21:1-8

Then I saw a new heaven and a new earth, for the first heaven and the first earth had passed away, and the sea no longer existed. I also saw the Holy City, new Jerusalem, coming down out of heaven from God, prepared like a bride adorned for her husband. Then I heard a loud voice from the throne: Look! God's dwelling is with humanity, and He will live with them. They will be His people, and God Himself will be with them and be their God. He will wipe away every tear from their eyes. Death will no longer exist; grief, crying, and pain will exist no longer, because the previous things have passed away. Then the One seated on the throne said, "Look! I am making everything new." He also said, "Write, because these words are faithful and true." And He said to me, "It is done! I am the Alpha and the Omega, the Beginning and the End. I will give water as a gift to the thirsty from the spring of life. The victor will inherit these things, and I will be his God, and he will be My son. But the cowards, unbelievers, vile, murderers, sexually immoral, sorcerers, idolaters, and all liars—their share will be in the lake that burns with fire and sulfur, which is the second death."

From this passage, you can see that everything in human history now comes full circle. The curse is lifted. The darkness is cast out. The evil is banished. And the end is even better than the beginning. Throughout the entire bible, we see the transformation of man.

We began in a sinless Garden.
We continue in a sanctified City.

We began in a place of Innocence.
We conclude in a place of Redemption.

> **John 14:1-3**
> *Your heart must not be troubled. Believe in God; believe also in Me. In My Father's house are many dwelling places; if not, I would have told you. I am going away to prepare a place for you. If I go away and prepare a place for you, I will come back and receive you to Myself, so that where I am you may be also.*

We are going *somewhere.* Just as certain as the fact that we came from somewhere, we know we are heading somewhere. So what do we do in the meantime?

One of the most famous followers of Jesus, named Paul, knew this and it changed the way he lived.

Phil 1:21-24

For me, living is Christ and dying is gain. Now if I live on in the flesh, this means fruitful work for me; and I don't know which one I should choose. I am pressured by both. I have the desire to depart and be with Christ—which is far better— but to remain in the flesh is more necessary for you

How does knowing you have a destiny affect how you live in the present?

What are some ways we could apply this phrase, "to live is Christ, and to die is gain"?

For some people, speaking the truth of God to others is the most natural and immediate response of faith. For example, the woman at the well in Samaria was so passion about witnessing, she left her pots and ran into the town. She engaged in evangelism after knowing Jesus for only a few minutes!

> **John 4:28-30**
> *Then the woman left her water jar, went into town, and told the men, "Come, see a man who told me everything I ever did! Could this be the Messiah?" They left the town and made their way to Him.*

For others, talking about Jesus to other people is a difficult task indeed. Either way, we are commanded to take our faith public. Here is one of the last things Jesus said to His disciples before ascending into heaven:

> **Acts 1:8**
> *But you will receive power when the Holy Spirit has come on you, and you will be My witnesses in Jerusalem, in all Judea and Samaria, and to the ends of the earth.*

Being a Christian means following Christ. Following Christ includes telling others about Him. We are witnesses of God's goodness and truth not only in how we speak but how we live.

Some of your old friends may think that you are strange and will gossip about you. Because of this, it is critically important to walk in the light so that they will see God in you.

> **I Peter 4:3-7**
> *For there has already been enough time spent in doing what the pagans choose to do: carrying on in unrestrained behavior, evil desires, drunkenness, orgies, carousing, and lawless idolatry. 4 So they are surprised that you don't plunge with them into the same flood of wild living—and they slander you. 5 They will give an account to the One who stands ready to judge the living and the dead. 6 For this reason the gospel was also preached to those who are now dead, so that, although they might be judged by men in the fleshly realm, they might live by God in the spiritual realm. 7 Now the end of all things is near; therefore, be serious and disciplined for prayer.*

The are three primary enemies that will try to prevent you from being a witness: Fear, Apathy, and Unbelief

1. I am afraid
2. I don't care
3. I do not believe

Talk to your mentor about each of these and rank them in order of most-to-least relevant. As you discuss a strategy with your mentor, they will help you put your evangelism into practice!

For more insight on how the scientific and philosophical investigation of the universe points to God, I have not found a better book than this one:

New Proofs for the Existence of God: Contributions of Contemporary Physics and Philosophy (Spitzer 2010)

On the philosophy of Christianity:

Mere Christianity (Lewis)

On the nature of God:

The Knowledge of the Holy: The Attributes of God: Their Meaning in the Christian Life (Tozer)

On the nature of Man and Heaven/Hell:

The Great Divorce (Lewis)